The Big Ideas Club Presents

Poetic Philosophy

Narrative Translations Designed for Accessibility

Kant's Critique of Pure Reason: A Martial-Judicial Toil-Of

By Emmanuel Kant

Translated by Jason Kassel, PhD

## Table of Contents

Glossary of Kant's Martial-Judicial Noun-Verbs

Below the noun-verbs are aligned with Kant's original German where applicable.  The terms are distinguished by domain (Judicial and Martial), the German source terms where Kant uses them (with *Critique of Pure Reason* citations), andtheir metaphorical function are described.

---

⚖️ Judicial Noun-Verbs (aligned with *Kant's Tribunal der Vernunft*)

| English Metaphor | German Source Term(s) | Citation / Function |
|---|---|---|
| Summons | *Aufforderung*, *Vorladung* (implied) | Kant speaks of appearances being called before Judgment (cf. *A xii, B xxxviii*) |

| Witness | *Zeuge* (rare, but implied in *Beisitzung*) | Reason testifies to its own forms (*B xiii*) |
| --- | --- | --- |
| Judge | *richten, Gericht* | "Tribunal der Vernunft" (*B xxxv*) |
| Bind | *verbindet, Verknüpfung, Verbindung* | Core term in synthesis and lawfulness (*B 130, A 77*) |
| Writ | *Gesetz, Urteil, Spruch* | Kant often uses *Gesetzgebung* metaphorically (law- |

| | | giving Reason) |
|---|---|---|
| Offering-of-Judgment | *Urteil, Angebot* (contextually inferred) | You translate "Urteil" (judgment) as an active "Offering"—consistent with *A 68* |
| Lawful-Construction | *gesetzmäßige Konstruktion, Erkenntnisform* | Construction under lawful rules (cf. *A 713/B 741*) |
| Mandate | *Gebot, Imperativ, Forderung* | Especially in the practical Critique; already implied in *B 110–111* |

| | | |
|---|---|---|
| Tribunal | *Tribunal, Gerichtshof* | Explicit phrase: *das Tribunal der Vernunft (B xxxv)* |
| Testify | *Zeugnis geben, Beweis führen* | Implied when Reason "proves" its method (*A xii*) |
| Jurisdiction | *Zuständigkeit, Umfang, Grenze* | Kant defines limits: *die Grenze der Erfahrung (A 760/B 788)* |
| Authorize | *Rechtfertigen, Befugnis, Gültigkeit* | Legitimacy of categories in Deduction (*B 116–122*) |

| | | |
|---|---|---|
| Exclusion | *Ausschluß, Absonderung, Begrenzung* | Used when denying illegitimate claims (*A 254/B 310*) |
| Courtroom | *Gericht, Verhandlung* (contextually) | You render Reason's arena as a "Court"—fair extrapolation from *Gerichtshof* |
| Hearing | *Anhörung, Verhandlung* (implied) | Metaphorical: appearances "heard" in Judgment |
| Appeal | *Berufung, letzte Instanz* | "Court of Last Appeal" mirrors *letzte* |

| English | German | Citation / Function |
|---|---|---|
| | | *Instanz der Vernunft* (cf. *B xxxv*) |
| Sentence | *Urteil, Ausspruch* | "Judgment" as both act and sentence (*A 68, B 90*) |
| Hold-in-Judgment | *Urteil fällen, in Gültigkeit setzen* | Holding a manifold under a judgment (*B 141*) |

---

⚔ Martial Noun-Verbs (aligned with *Kant's metaphors of struggle, discipline, formation*)

| English Metaphor | German Source Term(s) | Citation / Function |
|---|---|---|

| Deploy | *aufstellen, einsetzen, verwenden* | Kant's deployment of categories (*A 65–66*) |
| --- | --- | --- |
| Formation | *Bildung, Formierung* | Structural lawfulness of judgment (*A 79, B 104*) |
| Campaign | *Feldzug, Bemühung* | Kant uses *Bemühung* to describe failed attempts at metaphysics (*A ix*) |

| | | |
|---|---|---|
| Retreat | *zurückziehen, auf die alte Bahn zurück* | "Return to the old path" as metaphorical fallback (*A ix*) |
| Secure-Path | *sichere Gang, sichere Bahn* | Kant's core metaphor for science (*A viii, A x*) |
| Regiment | *Disziplin, Anordnung* | Implied in *Disziplin der reinen Vernunft* (*A 709/B 737*) |
| Ranks | *Reihe, Rangordnung* (implied) | "No step backward" = no broken ranks (*A x*) |

| | | |
|---|---|---|
| Withdraw | *zurückziehen, Rückzug* | Logic "has withdrawn no ranks" (*A x*) |
| Discipline | *Disziplin, Zucht* | Explicit in *Disziplin der reinen Vernunft* (*A 709*) |
| March | *Gang, Bahn* | Secure path = lawful march (*A viii–ix*) |
| Guard | *Bewachung, Sicherung* | Reason as guarding lawful limits (*A 760/B 788*) |

| | | |
|---|---|---|
| Flank / Stand-With | *Wechselwirkung, Nebenordnung* | Third Analogy: simultaneous interaction (*B 256*) |
| Command | *Befehl, Anweisung* | Implied in category application (*B 145*) |
| Overreach | *Überschreiten, Transgression* | Dialectic warns of overreaching Reason (*A 297/B 354*) |
| Collapse | *Zusammenbruch, Scheitern* | Systems fail, collapse without lawful |

| | | |
|---|---|---|
| | | grounding (*A viii–x*) |
| Fortify | *Befestigen, Fundieren, Absichern* | Securing structure in Deduction (*A 84–85*) |
| Drill | *Einübung, Disziplin* | Training of faculties (*A 709*) |
| Siege / Construction | *Konstruktion, Aufbau, Entwurf* | "Construction" is strategic and lawful (*A 713*) |

That-Which-Is-Highest Aesthetic

✗☐ Preface

Whether Toil-Of—
marshaling Knowledge
into a lawful formation—
Must-Count
as a Science
can be tested
by its result.

If,
after all deployments,
the structure stalls—
or
to reach its end,
Must-Retreat
and take another line—

Or
if no unification
can be forged
among Those-Toiling-in-the-Field-of-
Reason—

then we know:
What Must-Have-Been a Secure-Path
was only a Campaign of Wandering.

And what Feels-as-Though Science
is only Marching-in-the-Dark.

---

Only one **Toil-Of**
has ever held
to the **Secure-Path**
from the first deployment—
**Logic.**

Since **Aristotle**,
she has withdrawn no ranks,
made no retreat.
Her campaign is precise
because she asks nothing
of the world.

She does not reach
beyond the **Window**.
She governs only
the **Form of Judgment**—
not its content,
not its object,
not its weight.

Toil-Of **Logic**
measures **inward**,
remains **within jurisdiction**,

and never risks collapse—
because she never
**crosses the boundary**.

---

But **Reason**
is not content
to stay inside.

Her **Toil-Of**
does not end
at form.

She wants
to step beyond the frame—
to touch
what lies outside.

But when she does,
the **Path** breaks.
She must **retreat**,
**redraw**,
**try again**—

But every step
leads to **collapse**.

There is no agreement
among Toil-Of.

No single **structure**
that will **Hold**.

And so **Metaphysics**
does not walk
a **Secure-Path**.
It **wanders**.
It **circles**.
It **pretends to build**
where there is **no foundation**.

And **Reason**,
though driven to **Toil-Of**,
must face the truth:

She cannot **construct**
beyond what
**Must-Appear**
from within.

---

All Toil-Of**s** before
believed the **object**
must guide the **design**.

That **Knowledge**
must follow
**What-is-Given**.

But what if
that belief
was the reason
the **Secure-Path**
always **collapsed**?

What if
the **Object**
must follow
the **Form**?

What if the **world**
only **Must-Appear**
as Toil-Of
is structured
to **construct**?

Like **Copernicus**—
who stopped chasing stars
and let the **Earth** move instead—
**Toil-Of** now turns **inward**:

She does not **discover**
laws in the **world**.
She **legislates**
the world
through **lawful Form**.

What **appears**
does so
because the **Mind**
was already
structured
to make it **Appear**.

---

⚖ Opening of the Tribunal: *Toil-Of Builds and Stands Trial*

This is not
an **opinion**.
It is an **Experiment**.

**Toil-Of**
no longer seeks **proof**
in the **World**.

She **arranges**
the **structure**
so that what **Appears**
**Must-Fit**—
she draws the **Writ**.

If the **Path**
holds firm—
if what **Appears**
**aligns**

with what **Must-Be-There**
beforehand—

then **Reason**
 has **proven**
 her new method:

Not **passive observation**,
 but **lawful construction**.
 Not **imitation of the world**,
 but **Restriction**
 of what can **Appear**.

This is
 the **Court of Last Appeal**
 for **Appearances**—
 of **Pure Reason**.

And **Toil-Of**
 is both
 **Architect**
 and **Witness**.

---

The **Experiment**
 succeeds—
 but with a **cost**.

Yes, **Appearances**
**Must-Conform**
to the **Mind's design**.

But beyond **Appearance**,
**Reason** cannot **build**.
The **Structure** ends
at the **edge**
of what can be **Given**.

**Toil-Of**
cannot **cross**
into the **Thing-in-Itself**.
She may **gesture**,
but not **step**.

Every **Projection**
she draws
beyond the **Boundary**
collapses
into **Contradiction**.

She **reaches**—
**Beyond Must-Be limits**—
to **Draw the**
**Law of Postulate-Freedom -**
**(the stance of** Toil-Of on the far edge of what
May-Be-Lawful) -

to **Secure the Soul**,
to **Name a God**.

But these are not Edicts—
they are **Aspirations**.

No Charter grounds them.
No Tribunal can see them.

They are
**High-Symbols**
traced by Toil-Of
on the far edge
of what
**May-Be-Lawful.**

So **Reason**
must **stop**
at the **limit**
of what
**Must-Appear.**

Not because she is **weak**—
but because her **strength**
lies in what
she can **secure.**

Beyond that
is not **Knowledge**—
only **Longing**.

---

There is one **Jurisdictional-Space**
where **Reason** may step forward—
not in **Knowing**,
but in **Legislating**.

She cannot **know Postulate-Freedom -**
**That is, Toil-Of on the far edge of what**
 **May-Be-Lawful -**
But she must **act**
*as though* Postulate-Freedom
**Must-Be**.

And because she **Must-Act**,
The Law of Legislative-Reason dictates
She **Must-Legislate**.

This **Law**
 does not come from **outside**.
 No **God commands** it.
 No **object discloses** it.

It arises
 **from within**
 the structure

that **Reason herself**
**has legislated as Form**.

**Toil-Of**,
who could not **cross**
into the **Thing-in-Itself**,
now becomes
the **Legislator-of-Practical-Reason**.

Through the Law of Legislative Reason
The Legislator-of-Practical-Reason
Legislates that
the **Will Must-Conform**
to a Sovereign-**Law -**
**not a Natural-Law -**
it gives **to itself.**
Without these necessary fortifications,
**Morality** is contradictions of projections.

And so,
**Critique** ends not in **silence**,
but in the **sovereignty of**
the **Legislator-of-Practical-Reason**:
**Reason binds itself**
**in order to**
**Toil-Of on the far edge of what May-Be-**
**Lawful.**

## ⬚ Introduction

All Knowledge
 is judged
 not just by what it claims—
 but by **how it Comes-to-Appear.**

Its **Origin**
 matters as much
 as its outcome.

Is it born
 From-Experience?
 Or does it arise
 Before-Experience?

Some Knowledge
 is learned By-Observation.
 But some
 Appears-to-Structure
 which observation
 Must-Hold.

That is where
 the Critique begins.

Not with Objects,
 but with the **Form-of-Knowing**—
 with the ground

on which Toil-Of
 may lawfully begin to build
and defend
 its first fortress.

---

Every Judgment
 either **unfolds** what is already contained,
 or **adds** what was never there.

The first is called **Analytic**:
 Truth-by-Definition—
 a simple act of cutting open
 the concept
 and seeing what was inside.

The second is **synthetic**:
 Truth-that-**Puts-Together**—
 it reaches beyond
 the subject
 to grasp something new
And bring into the frame.

Analytic judgments
 are certain,
 but they build nothing.

Synthetic judgments
 are expansive—

but when based on experience,
they cannot be trusted to **Hold**.

What Toil-Of seeks
 is more rare:

A judgment that
Constructs-and-**Must-Hold**—
 even before experience.

This
 is the central task:

Can there be
 **synthetic judgments a priori**—
A Putting-Together-Grasping-
 the kind of Knowledge that both
expands and secures,
raising a Judgment-Fortress
strong enough to stand against all assaults?

A Judgment-Fortress built of:
Analytic stones
laid deep and sure,
Synthetic ramparts
that reach beyond,
and the final fortification —
Synthetic a priori —
which both constructs

and Must-Hold,
anchoring the whole
against the
Assaults-of-Doubt.

---

Synthesis
 is not Reflection.
 It is not Observation.

It is the act of
**Putting-Together-And-Grasping**
what was Apart—
of shaping
what alone
could never Hold.

Toil-Of
 does not inspect only.
 She combines.

She takes the Manifold—
 scattered, sensuous, unordered—
 and places it
 into structure.

This act of
**Putting-Together-And-Grasping**

does not arise from the world.
It comes from Within.
It is spontaneous.
It is blind,
but necessary.

Without **Putting-Together-And-Grasping,**
there is no Judgment-Fortress.
Without Judgment-Fortress,
there is no Knowledge.

Every Trial-of-Truth
begins
in this motion:

**Combine — Break — Judge.**

What appears
must be built
from parts
that do not yet
belong together—
but must
if anything
is to appear at all.

The Categories —
those pure Concepts-of-the-Understanding —
are tools
lying within the Judgment-Fortress.
Alone,
they guard nothing,
command nothing,
reveal nothing.
They are Forms
without motion —
walls without gates.

Only when the
scattered, sensuous, and unordered
Manifold
arrives as Raw-Offering,
does the Judgment-Fortress
open its Gate
to receive it.
In that moment,
Putting-Together-And-Grasping
brings the Manifold
under Sovereign-Form,
and secures
what alone
could never Hold.

Without Putting-Together-And-Grasping,
 the Categories are empty.

Without the Manifold,
 they are blind.

Toil-Of must not only possess the tools—
 she must use them
 **lawfully**,
 in the act of
 **Combine — Break — Judge.**

---

That-Which-Is-Highest Deduction

### ⚖️ Opening

#### 🎭 The Trial of Toil-Of's Tools

Toil-Of now faces
 the Tribunal of Reason.

She cannot simply
 reach for her tools
 and shape what appears.

She must **justify**
 the right
 to use them.

These Forms—
Quantity, Cause, Substance, Necessity—
are not self-evident.

They claim
to structure the world.
But what gives them
the power
to **Bind** what appears?

The Manifold
does not come marked
with structure.

It is Toil-Of
who places Form
upon it—
but now
she must show
that this act
is not arbitrary.

She must show
that without these Forms,
nothing
could **appear as appearance**
at all.

# ⬚ The Origin of Authority

## ☻ The Unity That Makes Judgment Possible

What gives Toil-Of
 the right
 to Form what appears?

What allows her
 to **Put-Together-And-Grasp**
 the manifold
 as one thing?

It is not memory.
 Not ego.
 Not presence.

It is the demand
 that every appearance
 Must-Be-Grasped
 as **for one Mind.**

This is called
 the **Unity-of-Grasping—**
 the condition that makes
 any act of building
 possible at all.

It is what allows
 one moment

to follow another
and still belong
to the same Offering.

It is not said aloud—
 but it is always written
 at the base of the structure:

*"I think."*

Not as proof—
 but as signature.

Without this Unity,
 the Manifold
 could never be held.

And without holding,
 there is no Judgment.
 No Knowledge.
 No world
 that Must-Appear.

---

## ⚔️ Lawful Application Begins

### 🎭 The Forms Are Now Bound to the Offering

The Mind
 cannot grasp

the Manifold
without Form.

But the Form
is not given—
it is applied
through Judgment.

And Judgment
is not passive—
it is Lawful.

When Toil-Of
unites the Manifold
under the Unity-of-Grasping,
the Categories
**Must-Bind**
that Offering
into structure.

Each Form—
Substance, Cause, Quantity—
becomes a condition
for the Offering
to even **appear as experience**.

This is not a system
imposed from outside.

It is the **inner legislation**
of Reason itself.

The Categories
are not floating tools.
They are the **Authorized Forms**
that Must-Be-Used
for Judgment
to occur at all.

If an Offering
is to Hold,
it must be shaped
by these Forms—
or it cannot
be recognized
as knowledge.

---

At this moment, the **Trial ends**:

- The Forms have been **justified**.

- Toil-Of may now **construct**.

- Judgment has its **jurisdiction**.

- What appears, must do so **lawfully**.

---

That-Which-Is-Highest Analytic

▢ *The Training Ground: §§1–§26*

📖 **§1 — Of Intuition in General**

Before Toil-Of can Judge,
 something
 Must-Appear.

But what appears
 is not yet thought.
 It is not concept.
 It is not structure.

It is the Offering—
 raw, singular, immediate.

It does not arise
 from within.
 It is given.
 But it is not the object—
 it is **the way**
 an object
 enters the Mind.

This Offering
is called **Intuition**.

And even Intuition
requires a frame.
It must be received
in a certain way—
a way
that can later
be Grasped.

The Mind
may Toil-Of,
legislate,
divide—
but it cannot **initiate**
what Intuition gives.

It can only accept,
shape,
and place.

Without Intuition,
the Mind
would build
from nothing.

## ■ §2 — *Von dem Raume*

Toil-Of
does not learn Space—
she **must already see**
**in** it.

Space
is not built from appearances.
It is what makes
appearance possible.

No object
gives her Space.
No sensation
teaches it.

Every outward Offering
must be received
in this Form—
as extended,
positioned,
separable.

Space is not discovered.
It is the silent structure
the Mind already
Must-Have

before anything
can Appear outside.

It is not a thing.
It is not a concept.
It is not even
in the world.

It is the **outer condition**
of anything being
shown as world.

Toil-Of cannot reach out
without it.
Even fantasy
must borrow its shape.

Space is the frame
through which
all motion is drawn,
all lines are measured,
all bodies appear.

But it is not one body among others.
It is the condition
for there to be
**bodies at all.**

## ◼ §3 — *Von der Zeit*

Toil-Of
does not see Time.
She **feels within it**.

Just as Space
shapes what appears
outside,
Time
shapes what unfolds
within.

She does not measure Time
by clocks.
She experiences
change,
order,
sequence.

Even without movement,
she senses succession.

Time is not taught
by experience.
It is what makes
experience move.

The dream,
the memory,
the echo—
all are only possible
because Time
**Must-Be-There**
as the form
of inner Offering.

No object
can escape it.
Even in Space,
everything Must-Appear
in Time.

And yet—
Time is not something
in the world.
It is the world's
inner law of becoming.

She cannot grasp
any appearance
without it.
Time is Toil-Of's
silent line—
always drawing,

always flowing,
never seen.

What lasts,
what follows,
what repeats—
all depend
on this invisible form.

---

## ■ §4 — The Schematism of the Pure Concepts of the Understanding

Vom Schematismus der reinen Verstandesbegriffe

Toil-Of holds
tools of pure Form—
Quantity, Cause, Substance, Necessity.

But the world
she must judge
does not stand still.
It flows.

Appearances arise
in Time—
stretched, fading,
ordered,

but never held
all at once.

How can a Form
so pure,
so timeless,
**grasp**
what is always
in motion?

There must be
a middle power—
a hidden hand
that draws time
into form.

This is called
the **Figure-of-Grasping**,
the unseen movement
that prepares
the Offering-for-Judgment.

It is not drawn
from experience.
It belongs to Toil-Of—
but not to the Concept.

It is not the law,
and not the material,

but the **rule**
that allows the law
to be applied.

Without this power,
the Categories
would remain
suspended—
unable to enter
what Must-Appear.

But with it,
the Offering
is made lawful—
appearances
are made fit
for Judgment.

This power
Toil-Of draws
from the Imagination—
not as fantasy,
but as **function**:

A silent, lawful movement
that aligns time
with form
so that Reason
may Judge.

# ■ §5 — *System of All Principles of Pure Understanding*

Judgment does not serve
what is already
**Contained-Within**.

That is not construction—
it is unfolding.

But Reason
must build.
And what it builds
always includes
what is
**Not-Contained-Within**
the concept alone.

This is not error.
It is necessity.

Judgment reaches outward—
and when it does so
in lawful form,
it **extends knowledge.**

These are the Principles
of the Court of Understanding.

They do not confirm
what was already there.
They declare
what Must-Hold
when the Offering
brings in more
than the concept alone.

Without these Principles,
no knowledge
beyond definition
would ever arise.

The Mind would remain
within itself—
folded, certain,
and empty.

---

## 📖 §6 — The Axioms of Intuition

### (*Die Axiome der Anschauung*)

Before Toil-Of
can measure,
compare,
or explain—

she must see
that something is **there.**

Not vaguely—
but **as magnitude**:
stretched, shaped,
extended
in the Form of Space
and drawn through Time.

This judgment
is not Contained-Within
the idea of "object."

It is **Not-Contained-Within**—
but arises from the way
appearances Must-Appear
to be grasped at all.

To judge anything
as present
requires
Putting-Together-And-Grasping
in intuition—
as a unity
of space and moment.

These are called
**Axioms**—

not because they are self-evident,

but because they are the

**bare structural minimum**

that must already Hold

before any further concept

can be applied.

They are what make

Quantity

possible at all.

Toil-Of

sees no number

until magnitude

is already there

to be measured.

And that magnitude

must be offered

in intuition

through lawful Form—

or nothing

can be judged

to exist.

---

## ■ §7 — Anticipations of Perception

Not all Offerings
are shape and size.

Some are light.
Some are warmth.
Some are force.

They do not
extend in space—
but they **intensify**
in time.

Toil-Of
cannot measure them
by width
or position.

And yet—
they Must-Be-Felt
as **more or less**,
as **present with weight**,
as **having tone**.

These Offerings
do not present a figure.
But they are not formless.

Their law
is not shape—
but **degree.**

What appears in quality
Must-Appear
as capable
of **greater or lesser.**

This judgment
is Not-Contained-Within
the concept of "sensation."

It must be Grasped
through a lawful frame—
the same Form
that carries Time.

Because the Offering
comes to us
in Time,
even quality
must unfold
in succession—
as gradation,
as rhythm,
as force that
Must-Be-There
**as varying intensity.**

This is the Principle:
Quality Must-Be-Felt
as **degree**
if it is to be judged
at all.

---

# ◼ §8 — The Analogies of Experience

The Offering
does not come
in pieces.

It comes
in time.

But Time
flows.
It does not stand.
It does not repeat.
It does not explain itself.

If Toil-Of
let it pass
without form—
there would be no knowledge.
Only sequence.
Only loss.

She must **Hold Time together.**

Not by freezing it—
 but by judging it
 **as relation.**

Three forms
 give Time structure:

◆ One that Holds—

**Substance**

(what endures through change).

◆ One that Follows—

**Cause**

(what must come after what).

◆ One that Stands-With—

**Reciprocity**

(what exists at the same time in lawful
relation).

These are not appearances.
 They are **judgments**
 about how appearances
 Must-Appear
 **in order to be experienced at all.**

Toil-Of
does not see these Forms—
she **must apply them.**

And they are not chosen.
They are what
Time
Must-Be-Fitted-Into
if the Offering
is to Hold.

---

## ■ §9 — Postulates of Empirical Thought in General

The Offering
may appear.
It may even Hold.
But what
does that mean?

To be seen
is not yet
to **exist.**

Toil-Of
must now Judge
not only what is formed—

but how it stands
before Reason.

Every Offering
must be tested
in one of three modes:

◈ Is it **Possible**?
—Can it be thought
in lawful form?

◈ Is it **Actual**?
—Is it given
in lawful appearance?

◈ Is it **Necessary**?
—Does its Being
follow from what Must-Be?

These are not categories.
They are **decisions**
the Mind Must-Make
in Judgment.

Toil-Of does not say:
"This is."

She must say:
"This **May-Be**,

"This **Is-There**,

"This **Must-Be**."

And she says it
 not based on feeling,
 but on how the Offering
 is Grasped
 in lawful time.

**Possibility** = Agreement with Form.
 **Existence** = Presentation in Time.
 **Necessity** = That which cannot
 Not-Be
 if all else Holds.

These are the **Postulates**.
 They allow Toil-Of
 to speak
 not just of shape, force, and relation—
 but of **Being**.

---

## 📖 §10 — *Refutation of Idealism*

Toil-Of
 is accused
 of dreaming.

"You see only inward."
"You construct appearances."
"There is no world—
only the play
of your categories."

But she replies:
"If only I appeared—
then I could not even
appear **to myself.**"

Inner experience
unfolds in Time.
But Time
has no line
without something
to Hold it.

And what Holds?
Not the self—
for it flows.

What must Hold
is something **outside**—
something stable,
something that endures
**while** the self
changes.

The very idea
 of inner succession
**Requires**
 the presence of
**outer permanence.**

If I am to know
 myself in time,
 then there Must-Be
 something
 that does not
 pass.

Idealism fails
 because it forgets
 this foundation:

The Mind
 cannot think
 the succession of its own Offering
 without first
**anchoring the line**
 in the world.

---

■ **§11 — On the Ground of the Distinction of Objects into Appearances and Things in Themselves**

Toil-Of
does not deny
that more may exist.

But she must now
**draw the boundary**
between
what may Appear
and what
must remain
**outside the Offering**.

What is judged
must be
in Space and Time.
These are the conditions
of the Court.

Whatever cannot
be given
in these Forms—
cannot be judged.

It may still
**Be There.**
But it cannot
Be Known.

These are called
**Things-in-Themselves**—
objects as they might be
**before they enter**
our Form.

But once they Appear,
they are no longer
in themselves.
They are now
**Appearances**—
shaped by our faculty
of receiving.

Toil-Of
does not deny
the Thing-in-Itself.
She simply says:
it lies **outside the Gate.**

Only what enters
through lawful form
may stand
before Judgment.

---

## 📖 §12 — Systematic Representation of All Principles of Pure Understanding

Toil-Of
has shown the tools.
She has tested them.
She has judged their reach.

Now she lays them out
in **System.**

Not as a stack—
but as a **house:**
joined, leveled, ordered
in relation to one another.

Each Category
receives its Principle.
And each Principle
Must-Hold
if experience
is to appear lawfully.

The ground
is **Time**—
and all structure
must rise
through its line.

This is not merely
table or taxonomy.
It is the full

**Architectonic**

of Judgment:

❧ **Quantity** → Axioms of Intuition

❧ **Quality** → Anticipations of Perception

❧ **Relation** → Analogies of Experience

❧ **Modality** → Postulates of Empirical Thought

Each is a way
 of saying what
 Must-Be-There
 for the Offering
 to be judged
 at all.

If any one
 were missing,
 the system would collapse.

But joined together,
 they form
 the lawful court
 of all experience.

---

■ **§13 — On the Fundamental Rule for the Use of the Principles in General**

Toil-Of
 has drawn the House.
 But how
 shall she apply it?

The Principles
 are not abstractions.
 They are Laws
 for **actual use**.

To be used,
 they must not only Hold—
 they must **Fit**
 what appears.

But appearances
 do not arrive whole.
 They arrive
 as flow,
 as change,
 as manifold—
 always in Time.

Time
 is the condition
 of all application.

The Forms
 must be applied

to what is **given in time**—
or they are not applied at all.

This is the **Fundamental Rule**:

> Every Offering
> Must-Appear
> as something
> **in time**
> if it is to be judged
> by the Principles.

No magnitude
can be seen
without succession.
No intensity
can be judged
without variation.
No relation
can be held
without a timeline.

The system
rests on one law:

**Time Holds All.**

Not because it is seen—
but because it is the form

through which
all else Must-Be-Drawn.

---

## 📖 §14 — First Analogy of Experience: Substance is That Which Persists Through All Time

Toil-Of
cannot judge
only by change.

If everything shifted,
flowed,
dissolved—
there would be
no structure
to hold the Offering.

The Court would collapse
into sensation.

But Judgment
requires
something stable.

Something
that does not change
when others do.

Something
that gives time
a backbone.

This is called
**Substance**.

Not a thing.
But a form
that **Must-Be-There**
in order for any change
to even appear
as change.

All variation
is judged
against what Holds.

Toil-Of does not sense
Substance—
she **judges**
that it Must-Hold
if anything
is to be compared,
altered,
or known
as enduring.

Without this judgment,
 succession would be collapse.
 No event would be anchored.
 Time would pass
 without form.

The First Analogy
 declares:

> **Something Must-Hold**
> **across time,**
> **or nothing**
> **can be said to change.**

---

## ■ §15 — Second Analogy of Experience: All Change Occurs According to the Law of Cause and Effect

Toil-Of
 sees motion.
 Sees shift.
 Sees the Offering change.

But what does that mean?

If change
 is to be judged,
 it must unfold
 **in a lawful order.**

Not just "this, then that"—
but:

"This came first,
   **and it made** that follow."

The Mind
 cannot see causality.
 It cannot sense necessity.

It must **Judge**:
 that what follows
 did so
**because it was made to.**

This is not perception.
 It is the structure
 of all perception.

Without this Form,
 time would collapse
 into disorder.

The Court declares:

> **All change**
> **Must-Follow**
> **the Law of Causality.**

Toil-Of
does not impose this—
she cannot help
but Judge this way
**if the Offering is to Hold.**

And if the Order
cannot be judged
as necessary,
then the event
cannot be called
experience.

---

### ▦ §16 — Third Analogy of Experience: All Substances, Insofar as They Are Regarded as Simultaneously Existing, Stand in Mutual Interaction

Toil-Of
has seen what Holds.
She has judged what Follows.

Now she must judge
what **Stands-With.**

For more than one substance
to be said to exist
at the same time,

they must
not just appear together—
they must
**interact.**

Not collide.
Not blend.
But be **judged**
**as standing**
**in lawful relation**
**within one Time.**

Time, on its own,
does not show simultaneity.
It flows.

To judge
that things coexist,
Toil-Of must
judge a world
of **reciprocity**—
where appearances
are not isolated,
but drawn together
by a shared structure.

This is **Community**:
the Form of **Mutual Relation**
that Must-Hold

if experience
is to include
more than one.

The Court does not say:
"I see two."
It says:

> "These two
> Must-Be-Together
> in one Frame
> or they cannot
> be judged real."

This is the Third Analogy:

**What Coexists
Must-Stand-In-Relation
within a shared Time.**

---

## ▪ §17 —Explanation of the Possibility of Experience in General Through the Three Analogies

Experience
is not given.
It is **made possible**
by Judgment.

But Judgment
 does not act beyond
the far edge of what May-Be-Lawful.
 It is bound
 to three conditions
 that must always Hold:

❧ **Something Must-Hold**

—so that time is not lost to change.

❧ **Something Must-Follow**

—so that time is not chaos.

❧ **Something Must-Stand-With**

—so that multiple things
may appear as part
of one world.

These are not
observations.
They are the **Forms**
that make observation
into experience.

Toil-Of
 does not ask
 what she sees—
 she asks:

"What Must-Hold
in order for
what I see
to be seen
at all?"

These three judgments
are not optional.
They are the beams
of the House of Experience.

They are not derived
from sense—
but make sense
into structure.

Without them,
there is no persistence,
no event,
no world.

---

### ■ §18 — On the Principles of Pure Understanding and the Possibility of That-Which-Is-Highest Cognition

Toil-Of
has learned to Judge.

The Court stands.
The Offering is structured.

But now she must ask:

> "Are there limits
>   to what may be judged?"

She does not ask this
 from ignorance.
 She asks it
 to protect the structure
 from collapse.

What can be Judged
 is what
 **Must-Appear**
 in Space and Time.

This is called
 **The-Graspable**.

Not because it is held already—
 but because it can be
 **Put-Together-And-Grasped**
 in lawful form.

But there is more.
 There is that
 which cannot

be brought
into the Offering.

Not because it is false—
but because it is
**That-Which-Cannot-Be-Grasped**.

It lies beyond
Space and Time.
It cannot be formed
by Imagination.
It cannot be judged
by the Categories.

It may be real.
It may even
Must-Be-There.

But it cannot enter
the House of Judgment.

This is not a flaw.
It is the Foundation:

> To Judge is to distinguish
> not only what Holds—
> but what must remain
> **outside the Gate**.

The Critique
  does not destroy
  That-Which-Cannot-Be-Grasped.
  It draws the line
  so that what **can** be grasped
  may Hold.

---

### ▣ §19 — On the Limit of the Application of Principles and the Possibility of That-Which-Is-Highest Illusion

  Toil-Of's tools
  are lawful.
  But they are not limitless.

  Their reach ends
  where the Offering ends—
  at the edge
  of Space and Time.

  But Reason
  is tempted.
  It seeks unity.
  It seeks the total.

  And sometimes,
  it tries to use
  what was built

for The-Graspable
on That-Which-Cannot-Be-Grasped.

It asks questions
beyond appearance.
It applies form
beyond the Offering.

And when it does,
something dangerous appears:

**That-Which-Is-Highest Illusion**—
not false perception,
but lawful form
**used unlawfully**.

The illusion
is not in the world.
It is in Toil-Of's own hands—
when she turns the tools
beyond the Gate.

And the illusion
feels lawful.
It moves with the rhythm
of correct Judgment.

But it is not
Grasping.

It is a shadow
cast by law
beyond where law
may speak.

The Court
must now judge
its own limits—
or it will create
the very error
it was built to prevent.

---

# 📖 §20 — On the That-Which-Is-Highest Illusion Regarding the Idea of the Soul

Toil-Of
turns her gaze inward.

She does not see
another Offering.
She sees
**the one who Grasped.**

But this
is where illusion begins.

For now, Reason
tries to judge

**itself**
as if it were
another thing.

It uses its own Form—
unity, substance, cause—
not to judge appearances,
but to judge
**the Grasper.**

And so, it says:

"I am one."
"I do not change."
"I endure forever."

These are not facts.
They are **forms**
mistaken for facts.

They arise not from
That-Which-Was-Given,
but from
**the act of Grasping itself**.

The illusion is subtle.
Reason confuses
the necessary unity
of apperception

with the idea
of an immortal soul.

But what holds
Judgment together
**cannot itself**
be made
the Offering.

What Grasped
**cannot be Grasped**
**in the same way.**

The Soul
as object—
as something eternal, simple, indivisible—
is not The-Graspable.

It is a shadow
of Judgment
caught
in the mirror
of Toil-Of's hand.

---

## ■ §21 — On the That-Which-Is-Highest Illusion Regarding the World as Totality

Toil-Of
 looks not just inward,
 but outward—
 and she asks:

    "What is the Whole?"

She sees motion.
 She sees relation.
 She sees the Offering change.

But still she longs.
 She wants to Grasp
 not only what is given—
 but **all** that could be given.

She asks:

    "Did it begin?"
    "Will it end?"
    "Is the world infinite?"

These are not questions
 of judgment.
 They are questions
 of **reach**.

And here
 the illusion begins.

For Time
 does not show the world.
 It allows only
 **moments to be plucked.**

The Offering
 is never complete.
 It is a string
 stretched under Judgment,
 and each event
 is a note
 **plucked into being.**

But Reason mistakes
 the sound
 for the instrument.

It takes what was plucked
 and imagines
 it could hold
 the whole melody
 in its hand.

This illusion—
 that the World
 can be grasped
 **as total—**
 is not false perception.

It is structure
used beyond its range.

The World
is not The-Graspable
as a Whole.

It is offered
one pluck at a time—
and each must be judged
in sequence.

To pretend otherwise
is to turn
what is lawful
into projection—
and to cast Reason
back into shadow.

---

## ▪ §22 — On the That-Which-Is-Highest Illusion Regarding a Necessary Being

Toil-Of
has judged the Offering.
She has drawn the System.
She has faced her limits.

But still—
there is one more thing
she wants to Grasp.

Not a soul.
Not a world.
But the Source.

She says:

"There must be
something that cannot
Not-Be."

A Being
without conditions.
A Ground
without origin.
A Cause
without before.

And so she reaches—
not to sense,
not to time,
but to **Being itself.**

This is where Reason
commits its boldest act:

It tries to **pluck the Absolute**
from nothing but
the structure
of its own judgment.

The Ontological Proof
is not a deduction.
It is a projection:

"If I can think the idea
of a necessary being—
it must exist."

But what is this
but a form
mistaken for content?

Existence
is not contained
within the concept.
It is not drawn
from logic.
It is never
Contained-Within.

Toil-Of
cannot pluck Being
from Thought.

She cannot
 Grasp the Absolute
 simply because
 she **needs** it
 to complete the system.

This is the final illusion:
 That what is **most needed**
 must therefore **be.**

But nothing
 was offered.

And the fruit
 was not meant
 to be taken.

---

### ■ §23 — On the Regulative Use of the Ideas of Pure Reason

Toil-Of
 stands at the edge.
 She has touched
 That-Which-Cannot-Be-Grasped.

And she does not destroy it.
 She does not deny it.
 She steps back—

and learns
how to use it
**without misuse.**

The Ideas
of Reason—
Soul, World, God—
are not Offerings.

They are not to be judged.
They are not to be grasped.

But they **guide.**

Not as tools—
but as lines
Toil-Of aims toward.

Not legislative—
**regulative.**

The Idea of the Whole
reminds her
to join each Offering
in lawful sequence.

The Idea of the Self
reminds her
that the judgment
must hold as one.

The Idea of the Absolute
reminds her
that Reason seeks unity—
not possession.

These Ideas
are not things.
They are **directions**.

Not roads to walk,
but **stars to steer by.**

Reason, when disciplined,
uses them not to conquer
That-Which-Cannot-Be-Grasped—
but to hold together
**The Graspable**,
so the system
may stand.

---

### ■ §24 — On the Empirical Use of the Pure Understanding and the Possibility of Experience in General

Toil-Of
has looked beyond.
She has reached

toward the Source.
She has seen
what must not be taken.

Now she returns
to what is given:
appearances
offered in time.

Judgment does not begin
with the total,
or the soul,
or the infinite.

It begins
where the Offering is **plucked.**

It begins
in what is shown
in Space and Time—
in what is lawfully given
to be judged.

The Categories—
Quantity, Quality, Relation, Modality—
are not forms of dreaming.
They are the structures
that allow Reason
to speak at all.

And they apply
 not beyond the Gate,
 but to that
 which is **Graspable.**

Every experience
 that may be called real
 arises only
 when these forms
 are joined
 to the Offering.

This is not restriction.
 It is power.

The Court
 cannot rule the heavens.
 But within its walls
 it speaks with clarity.

What is offered
 may be judged.
 And what is judged
 may Hold.

---

### 📖 §25 — How Experience Is Possible at All

Toil-Of
does not discover experience.
She builds it.

Not from matter.
Not from sensation.
But from the act
of **Grasping**.

The Offering
is plucked
in time.

But unless it is
Put-Together-And-Grasped,
it is nothing more
than a note
that fades.

Experience is the name
not for what appears—
but for what
is **held together**
by Form.

The Manifold
does not unite itself.
It is drawn
through Time,

and shaped
by Categories.

Toil-Of does not
collect impressions.
She judges Offerings
in sequence—
forming what Must-Hold.

This is how
experience is possible:

> A note plucked
> becomes an Offering.
> An Offering judged
> becomes a Moment.
> A sequence of Moments
> becomes a World.

Without this
there is no knowledge.
No continuity.
No sense.

Only fragments.
Only tones
that vanish
before they are joined.

## ■ §26 — Transition to the That-Which-Is-Highest Dialectic

Toil-Of
has completed the frame.
Every Offering
that may be judged
has its form.

Space and Time
have been grounded.
Form and Function
have been joined.
The System
may now stand.

Every principle
has been shown
to arise
from what is given—
and from how
it Must-Be-Grasped.

But now the Critique
must take up
a different task.

Not the formation
of knowledge—

but the **temptation
of Reason.**

For Reason
 does not rest
 in the lawful.
 It seeks the whole.
 It points
 beyond the Offering.

It wants not just
 The-Graspable,
 but That-Which-Cannot-Be-Grasped.

And it plucks
 from silence—
 weaving structure
 where no Offering
 was ever given.

The Court of Judgment
 must now become
 the Critique of Illusion.

It must learn
 where Reason reaches
 **past its right**,
 and where

that reaching
must be checked.

The path ahead
leads not through experience,
but through the shadow
of its form.

And if Reason
cannot hold itself
within the Gate,
then even what was lawful
may collapse.

The gavel is placed down.
The Trial of Judgment ends.

And now begins
the Trial of Reason
**against itself.**

That-Which-Is-Highest Dialectic

# Book I: The Concepts of Pure Reason

*⚖ The Courtroom Opens: §§27–§33*

## ▣ §27 — *Von der Idee der reinen Vernunft*

Reason does not stop
when Judgment is complete.

Toil-Of, having ruled
on all that may be offered,
now lifts her eyes
and asks:

"What lies beyond?"

She no longer seeks
an object in time—
but **unity itself**.

Not the kind
that Holds an Offering,
but the kind
that gathers all judgment
under one direction.

This is the first mark
of **Pure Reason**:
It reaches not for appearances—
but for **Ideas**.

And what is an Idea?
It is not a concept
drawn from experience.
It is not an image
that can be built.

It is a direction—
a **structuring pull**
that guides the system
toward a Whole
that can never be
completely offered.

Ideas are not judged.
They are not plucked.
They are **posited**—
as if there were
something final
toward which
all judgment bends.

The Soul.
The World.
The Absolute.

These are not known.
They are **postulated**—
**That-Which-Cannot-Be-Grasped**

but still shapes
Toil-Of's work.

Reason here
  does not legislate.
  It draws lines
  toward the Infinite—
  not to possess it,
  but to orient
  what can be built.

---

## ◼ §28 — On Pure Reason as the Seat of That-Which-Is-Highest Illusion

Reason
  does not create knowledge.
  It orients the Mind
  toward unity.

It seeks not the next Offering—
  but the **Whole**
  in which all offerings
  might one day be joined.

It is, by nature,
  a **Compass**—

always turning
toward That-Which-Cannot-Be-Grasped.

This is not an error.
It is a necessity
of its form.

But the illusion begins
when Toil-Of
mistakes this orientation
for judgment.

When she follows
the Compass
and believes
she has arrived.

The **That-Which-Is-Highest Illusion**
arises when the line drawn
for orientation
is mistaken
for a path that has been walked.

This illusion cannot be silenced.
It belongs to Reason's motion.
But it **must be Critiqued**.

And to Critique—
is not to negate.

It is to judge,

  to separate,

  to trace the lawful boundary

  between what the Compass

  may point toward

  and what Toil-Of

  may Grasp.

The Compass may remain.

  Its pull may be honored.

  But Toil-Of must know:

> "To orient is not to possess.
>
>   To desire is not to judge.
>
>   To critique is to draw
>
>   the lawful limit
>
>   of Reason's reach."

---

## Book II: The Dialectical Inferences of Pure Reason
### Chapter I: The Paralogisms of Pure Reason

### 📖 §29 — Introduction to the Paralogisms of Pure Reason

The Compass

  turns inward.

Not toward the world,
 but toward the Self.

It begins to trace
 the line of thought—
 not to judge appearances,
 but to find
 its own origin.

But a Compass
 does not draw itself.
 It is moved.

It turns
 around a point
 it did not place—
 a center
 it cannot see.

And now Reason,
 forgetting the hand
 that moved it,
 looks down
 at the circle
 and says:

   "There—this must be me."
   "This is unity."

"This is substance."
"This is the Soul."

But nothing was offered.
 No appearance in time.
 No pluck.
 No form.
 Only the trace
 of lawful motion.

Reason mistakes
 the act of Grasping
 for a thing
 that has been grasped.

This is the illusion
 of the Paralogism.

Not a false step in logic—
 but the lawful use
 of judgment
 **in a place with no Offering.**

The unity of apperception—
 which Must-Hold
 for judgment to be possible—
 is not itself
 a Graspable being.

The Compass
  is not the point.
  And the circle
  is not the hand.

Critique must now intervene:
  not to reject the Self,
  but to say:

  "This form cannot be judged.
  It was not offered.
  You have drawn a perfect arc—
  but the center
  lies outside the Gate."

---

■ §30 — First Paralogism: The Simplicity and Substantiality of the Soul

The Compass moves
  without contradiction.
  The I think
  accompanies every thought.

And Reason draws from this:

  "Then the Self
  must be **one**."

"It must be **simple**."

"It must be **substance**."

But nothing
 has been plucked.
 There is no appearance
 of the Soul.
 No measurement.
 No shape.
 No interaction.

Only the **form**
 that thought Must-Hold
 in order to think.

The Paralogism arises
 from a kind of
 **structural mimicry**:

   The form of unity
    is mistaken
    for a thing that is one.

And because no division
 is observed,
 Reason asserts:

   "Then no division
    is possible."

But absence of appearance
is not evidence of indivisibility.

A **simple substance**
is not shown.
It is declared
from the structure
of how thought moves.

Toil-Of
has judged unity—
not simplicity.
She has drawn motion—
not mass.

Critique steps in
not to shatter the claim,
but to ask:

"Has anything been offered
that allows you to say
this unity is a substance?"

The answer:
Nothing has appeared.
The point was never given.

The Compass was moved.
But the Hand remains unseen.

## ◼ §31 — Second Paralogism: On the Personal Identity of the Soul

Reason observes:
the thought "I think"
appears in every moment.

It judges this sequence
as unified.

And from this unity,
it claims:

"The Self
must be **one and the same**
through all time."

But this inference
is drawn from motion—
not from any Offering.

There is no
appearance of the Soul.
There is no
plucked moment
that says:

"This subject endures."

Only the **form**
  by which experiences
  are held together.

Toil-Of
  does not see a Self.
  She sees
  the line of appearances
  judged **as mine**—
  but never **shown**
  as one and the same.

The Paralogism arises
  when Reason confuses
  the necessary **form of attribution**
  with the **substance of a person.**

The Compass turns.
  Its needle returns.
  But the center
  has never been placed.

Continuity of claim
  does not prove
  identity of being.

Critique intervenes:

"You have drawn
a lawful line.
But you have not shown
that it belongs
to a single thing."

The Self is not
the object of time.
It is the condition
under which
time becomes legible.

The illusion here
is not false memory—
but **structural confusion**:
the idea that because the thread
must be woven together,
the weaver must be
**always the same.**

---

## 📖 §32 — Third Paralogism: The Distinctness of the Soul as a Substance from Matter

Reason now claims:

"The Soul is different
from anything material."

Why?
Because the Soul
is thought to be simple,
and matter
is extended, divisible,
changeable.

But where
is the Offering?

Has there been a moment
where the Soul
and the Body
stood before Judgment—
as appearances?

There has not.

The distinction is drawn
**between two shadows**.

One is a postulate:
the Soul,
simple and enduring.

The other:
a conception of matter
formed not from sense,
but from opposition.

And because they differ
  in structure,
  Reason draws a line—
  and calls it **real**.

But Toil-Of knows:

> "To draw a line
>   between two things
>   is to Judge.
>   And no judgment
>   may be passed
>   without something Offered."

The Compass here
  spins in abstraction.
  It marks a border
  on a map
  no one has walked.

The Paralogism is this:

> "I cannot conceive
>   the Soul
>   as material—
>   therefore it is
>   essentially different."

But **inconceivability**

is not a warrant.

Absence of concept

is not presence of truth.

Critique does not deny

the Soul.

It denies

the border.

> "If you draw a wall
>
> between two things,
>
> but neither has appeared,
>
> you have only
>
> separated
>
> your assumptions."

---

## ■ §33 — Fourth Paralogism: On the Soul's Supposed Independence from the World

Toil-Of

reaches its final claim:

> "I am known
>
> directly.
>
> The world,
>
> only indirectly.

Therefore, I am
more certain
than what surrounds me."

This is the Paralogism
 of Independence.

It speaks not from logic,
 but from **priority**—
Reason's desire
to ground itself
in something
untouched.

But Critique demands:

"What was offered?"

Was there a moment
 when the Self
 appeared without form?
Without time?
Without condition?

There was not.

The "I"
 that claims independence
 is still shaped
 by Time,

bound by Sequence,
judged in Form.

What appears inwardly
is no less shaped
than what appears
in Space.

Toil-Of
builds its illusion
by assuming
that what is not
spatial
must therefore be
unconditioned.

But the Inner-Offering
Is as Bound-By
the **far edge** of what **May-Be-Lawful**
than the Outer.

And to say:

> "I am more certain
> of myself
> than the world"

is to forget
that **certainty**

is not appearance—
it is **judgment**.

And all judgment
Must-Be-Drawn
through lawful form.

Toil-Of
is never free-floating.
It works
within the system
it claims to transcend.

This is the final Paralogism:
the illusion that Reason
may stand alone
while still moving.

But motion
requires ground.
And even Toil
must be carried
by the Frame.

---

⬛ *The Battlefield of the World: §§34–§38*

■ **§34 — Introduction to the Antinomy of Pure Reason**

Toil-Of
 has tried to grasp
 the Self.
 It has traced the circle
 around an invisible point.

Now it turns outward again.

Toward the **World.**
 Not as appearance—
 but as **Totality.**

It asks:

    "Is the world finite?"
     "Was there a first cause?"
     "Can Toil-Of on the far edge of what
       May-Be-Lawful exist?"
     "Is there a necessary being?"

These are not questions
 of judgment.
 They are the Compass
 pointing toward **completion.**

But now, something different occurs.
 For every question,
 Reason provides two answers:

One says **Yes.**
One says **No.**

And both are built
with equal law.

This is the Antinomy.
A war between lines
traced lawfully—
each ending
in contradiction.

Toil-Of
does not err.
It proceeds by rule.
But its rule
is being stretched
past the Offering.

And when the line
exceeds the frame,
it tears itself in two.

This is not illusion.
It is **conflict**
born from Reason's attempt
to legislate
where it was only meant
to orient.

Critique must now enter
the battlefield—
not to take sides,
but to ask:

"What is being judged here?
Was anything
truly offered?"

For when nothing
has been given,
even the best-built
judgment
may collapse
into paradox.

---

### 📖 §35 — The First Antinomy of Pure Reason

Toil-Of
asks its first great question:

"Did the world begin?"

The Compass points forward—
and also back.

And Reason draws
**two lawful lines:**

**Thesis:**

"The world must have a beginning.

Otherwise, infinity

would already be completed.

And infinity

cannot be finished."

**Antithesis:**

"The world cannot have a beginning.

For if it began,

what came before?

Nothing?

Then from nothing—something?

This too cannot be."

Both are lawful.

Both are Reason's work.

And yet—

**each undoes the other.**

This is the first

**Conflict-of-Law(s):**

Reason, when applied

to That-Which-Cannot-Be-Grasped,

divides against itself.

Toil-Of does not falter.
It proceeds by rule.
But the rule is now stretched
**past the Offering**.

Time, as form of appearance,
may be plucked—
but not **held as whole**.

Toil-Of assumes
a **totality of time**
as if it had been offered—
and then judges it
from within the Offering.

This is the fallacy:

> Applying judgment
> to the Whole
> as if it were
> a part.

Critique intervenes:

> "No contradiction lies
> within the world
> as offered.
> The contradiction arises

when you treat the Compass's pull
as the Gift itself."

What Reason here grasps
is not an answer—
but the shadow
of its own striving.

---

### ■ §36 — The Second Antinomy of Pure Reason

Toil-Of
turns to Space.
It asks:

> "Is matter made of parts
> that cannot be divided?
> Or can it always
> be broken down?"

Again, Reason draws
two lawful lines:

**Thesis:**

> "There must be simple parts.
> Otherwise, no whole
> could ever be built.

Infinite division
would dissolve all form."

**Antithesis:**

"There are no simple parts.
For any body,
however small,
can be thought as extended—
and what is extended
can be divided again."

Both sides
hold logic.
Both lines
follow law.

But again—
**each undoes the other.**

This is the second
**Conflict-of-Law(s).**

Toil-Of
tries to judge
the **whole of matter**—
but again forgets:

Only what is plucked
may be judged.

There is no appearance
of **the smallest**.
There is no Offering
of the infinite line.

These are concepts
born not from experience—
but from **Reason's need**
for completion.

And so Reason,
pulled by the Compass,
once again overreaches.

It demands a totality
that **never entered**
the Frame.

Critique must speak:

> "The divisibility of the Offering
> is a judgment made
> within experience.
> But what you now seek
> is the end of the line—
> or its endlessness—
> and this was never shown."

"The contradiction
lies not in matter—
but in Reason's act
of trying to hold
what was only
meant to orient."

---

### ■ §37 — The Third Antinomy of Pure Reason

Toil-Of
strains now
at its own foundations.

It asks:

"Is everything determined
by prior cause?
Or is there a first act
that is Toil-Of on the far edge of what
May-Be-Lawful?"

Reason again splits:

**Thesis:**

"There must be
Toil-Of on the far edge of what
May-Be-Lawful.

If every cause is determined,
then nothing begins.
There must be a first motion—
not caused,
but chosen."

**Antithesis:**

"There is no
Toil-Of on the far edge of what
   May-Be-Lawful.
Every act
must follow a cause.
Otherwise, law collapses.
The world becomes
chaos and miracle."

Both lines are lawful.
Both are drawn
by the Compass.

This is the third
**Conflict-of-Law(s).**

But now
the fracture cuts deeper—
not into what appears,
but into how

Toil-Of
might live.

For without
Toil-Of on the far edge of what    May-Be-
Lawful,
  there is no Responsibility.
  Without Law,
  there is no Coherence.

The Compass cannot point
  to both.

And yet—
  each line
  is built from reason's own structure.

Critique must pause here:

> "Experience cannot decide.
>   For Toil-Of on the far edge of what
>     May-Be-Lawful
>   is not offered
>   in appearance.
>   And Necessity is not seen
>   from within."

> "The contradiction
>   is not in what is judged—

but in what Reason
wishes to claim
without judgment."

Toil-Of
cannot collapse.
It must be held
within a **higher tension**—
a double line
that does not resolve,
but **must-be-held-together**.

---

### 📓 §37 — The Third Antinomy of Pure Reason

Toil-Of
now moves at once
**inward and outward**.

It asks:

> "Must every act
> follow from another—
> by law?"

Or:

> "Can there be
> a First Cause

that begins

from nothing but

**One's-Own-Law**?"

Again, Reason splits:

**Thesis**:

"There must be

Toil-Of on the far edge of what

  May-Be-Lawful.

  For if everything follows

  from what came before,

  then nothing ever begins.

  To act is to initiate.

  There must be

  One's-Own-Law."

**Antithesis**:

"There can be no

Toil-Of on the far edge of what

  May-Be-Lawful.

  Every event must be caused.

  Without causal law,

  the world collapses."

"Toil-Of on the far edge of what

  May-Be-Lawful

breaks.
One's-Own-Law sequences—
and gives the law
that law alone
could never begin."

This is the third
**Conflict-of-Law(s)**—
not of appearance,
but of Will.

Toil-Of
does not abandon the system.
It strains it.

It must hold together
both lines:

> The demand for law
> and the need to begin
> from **One's-Own-Law**.

This contradiction
does not arise from illusion.
It arises from
the **structure of Reason**
itself—
when it tries to **act**
while still obeying.

Critique must speak:

> "What you now seek
> is not a thing,
> but a condition.
> Not an Offering—
> but the **ground of offering.**"

> "You cannot see
> One's-Own-Law.
> But you must act
> as if it is
> the source."

Toil-Of
may never Grasp it—
but it must **orient by it.**

Toil-Of on the far edge of what    May-Be-
Lawful
is not shown.
But it is the silence
by which
the Compass turns.

---

■ **§38 —The Fourth Antinomy of Pure Reason**

Toil-Of
seeks its ground.
The frame has held.
The Compass has spun.
But now it asks:

"Is there something
that Must-Be?"

Not in time.
Not in sequence.
But as the **unconditioned cause**—
the final **because.**

And again, Reason splits:

**Thesis**:

"There must be
a Necessary Being.
Without it,
the chain of causes
never begins.
There is no end
without a ground
that does not move."

**Antithesis**:

"There can be
no Necessary Being.
Every concept
must be conditioned.
Every being
must be part of a chain.
To place a final cause
is to break the law."

Again—both are lawful.
Again—each destroys the other.

This is the fourth
**Conflict-of-Law(s)**.

And now the contradiction
touches the **Absolute**:

Toil-Of
longs for a **foundation
that will not shift**.
But the Compass
cannot point
to what was never shown.

What appears
is always conditioned.
And what is unconditioned
**does not appear.**

Toil-Of
wants both:

>A Being that Must-Be—
>and a World
>that obeys.

But to declare
a Necessary Being
is to assert presence
where none
has been offered.

And yet,
to deny it
is to sever
the line that Reason
cannot stop tracing.

Critique must say:

>"The contradiction
>does not lie in Being—
>but in the wish
>to place the Compass's pull
>into the frame
>of Judgment."

"You have reached
  the outermost tension:
  That-Which-Cannot-Be-Grasped
  now stands
  beneath every motion
  of Toil-Of."

"And still—
  no Offering
  has been made."

---

*▢ The Compass Realigns: §§39–§44*

## ▣ §39 — On the Ideal of Reason

Toil-Of
  has reached the edge.
  The contradictions
  have all been drawn.
  Each lawful line
  has met its mirror.

But Reason
  does not rest in collapse.
  It begins again.

Not with a new Offering—
 but with a new **construction**:

>  "What if there were
>  a Being
>  that Must-Be?
>  Not by proof—
>  but by necessity?
>  Not as appearance—
>  but as Form itself?"

Toil-Of
 does not imagine this Being
 from the senses.

It shapes it
 from the idea of **completeness**—
 drawing together
 all that would make
 a thing final:

Unity.
 Causality.
 Necessity.
 Perfection.

Not from any Offering—
 but from the **internal demand**
 to **close the system**.

This Ideal
　is not plucked.
　It is not judged.
　It is not conditioned.

It is shaped
　by Reason's own form—
　by the need
　for That-Which-Must-Complete.

A figure,
　not a being.
A horizon,
　not a point.

And yet—
　Toil-Of treats it
　as if it were real.

Critique must ask:

　　"Was this Offered?
　　Or only built
　　from longing?"

　　"Do you construct
　　out of structure?
　　Or out of fear
　　that without this Form,

your foundation
will shift beneath you?"

The Ideal is not
That-Which-Is.
It is That-Which-Is-Needed
for the Whole
to feel as if
it Holds.

But need
is not presence.
And Form
is not Offering.

---

### ■ §40 — On the Existence of a Supreme Being

Toil-Of
has shaped its Ideal—
Formed from necessity,
perfected by logic,
held together
by the longing
for That-Which-Must-Be.

But it is not enough
to point.

Not enough
to orient.

Toil-Of now asks:

> "Can this Being exist?"
> "Must it exist?"
> "If I can think it—
> is it already there?"

The Compass,
having drawn the Figure,
now wants to **stand upon it**.

Reason reaches
for the **Ontological Proof**:

> "If the idea of the Supreme Being
> contains all perfection,
> and if existence
> is a perfection—
> then existence
> must belong to the Being
> by necessity."

But here
Critique raises its voice.

It does not scorn the longing.
It does not deny the Form.

But it draws
the boundary:

> "Existence
> is not a predicate.
> It adds nothing
> to the concept.
> It is not perfection—
> it is presence."

> "And presence
> cannot be built
> from Thought."

Toil-Of
has confused Form
with Offering—
necessity
with actuality.

The Compass
is not a foundation.
The line it draws
cannot become
the stone it seeks.

What is thought
may orient.

What is longed for
may structure.

But nothing
**Must-Be**
simply because
it is needed.

Critique does not destroy
the Supreme Being.
It refuses to **possess**
what was only
drawn.

> "You may hold the Form
> as Ideal.
> You may act
> as if it orients all.
> But you may not
> claim it exists—
> unless it has been
> Offered."

---

### ■ §41 — On the That-Which-Is-Highest Ideal

Toil-Of
shaped the Ideal.

It drew the Figure
of the Necessary—
not from Offering,
but from inward Form.

And now
The Skill-Of-Judging-Lawfully
reveals what it is:

Not a Being.
Not a Ground.
Not a proof.

But a **projection**:
the reflection
of Reason's longing
for closure.

The Ideal is formed
by gathering all that must-be
for something to feel complete—
and shaping it
into **One**.

That **One**
is not grasped.
It is not present.

It is the **name**
that Reason gives
to its own need
for unity.

Toil-Of
misread the Figure.
It took the shape
as substance.
The frame
as foundation.

But now,
The Skill-Of-Judging-Lawfully
separates the lines:

    "This Ideal
    did not arrive
    from outside.
    It arose
    from within."

    "It is Reason
    folding back
    into Form—
    not Reason
    discovering
    That-Which-Must-Be."

The That-Which-Is-Highest Ideal
 is not false.
 It is not illusion.

It is the final trace
 of the Compass
 in lawful motion.

But it may not be judged
 as if it were Offered.
 It may only
 orient.

And its power lies not
 in what it reveals—
 but in what it prevents:

> **The collapse
> of Reason
> into pieces.**

---

Book III – **The Regulative Use of the Ideas of Pure Reason**

## ■ §42 — Introduction to the Regulative Use

Toil-Of
  has strained
  to the edge of what can be Grasped.

It tried to build
  a ground from longing.
  It tried to turn
  Form into Fact.

But now
  the Compass must be held differently.

The Skill-Of-Judging-Lawfully
  steps forward—not to deny Reason's reach,
  but to **repurpose it**.

The Ideas—
  Soul, World, God—
  do not disappear.

They return
  as **Rules**.

Not rules of judgment—
  but rules of **orientation**.

Toil-Of must still act.
  It must investigate.
  It must extend lines
  beyond the Offered—

not to believe them,
but to **structure the search**.

These Ideas
become **regulative**.

They guide
the building of knowledge
without ever claiming
that their Forms
are real.

The Ideal of Reason
becomes the scaffolding
of Inquiry.

And the Skill-Of-Judging-Lawfully
affirms:

> "That-Which-Cannot-Be-Grasped
> may still structure
> how we ask."

> "The Compass
> may draw arcs
> not to land—
> but to prevent
> the collapse of structure."

Thus the Ideas
remain—not as beings,
but as **limits**
and **aims**.

They protect
the motion of Reason
from tearing itself apart.

---

## ■ §43 — System of the That-Which-Is-Highest Ideas

Toil-Of
has stepped back
from the edge.

It no longer reaches
to grasp the Absolute.

Instead,
it begins to shape
the lines
by which Reason
may still move lawfully.

The Compass
does not rest.
But now it draws

not boundaries—
but internal order.

The Skill-Of-Judging-Lawfully
takes up
the three great Ideas:

◻ **Soul** – the Idea of the complete Subject
◻ **World** – the Idea of the totality of Conditions
◻ **God** – the Idea of the Unconditioned Unity

None are offered.
None are present.

But each
must orient a direction
of Reason's striving.

Together they form
a **System**.

Not a map of what is—
but a structure
that holds Reason
from falling inward.

Without these Ideas,
Toil-Of collapses
into fragments—

disconnected,
directionless.

The Ideas are not walls.
They are beams—
invisible supports
that span
what cannot be grasped.

And each
must be used
not as Truth—
but as **Regulative Form**.

The Skill-Of-Judging-Lawfully affirms:

> "They give us
> no content—
> but they structure
> the lawful unfolding
> of content."

> "The System
> is not known—
> but it Must-Hold
> for knowing
> to continue."

### ■ §44 — On the Final Aim of the Natural Conflict of Human Reason

Toil-Of
 has strained
 to hold the world together.

It pulled the lines
 of Reason
 until they tore.

It spun the Compass
 until its points
 conflicted.

But now—
 The Skill-Of-Judging-Lawfully
 reveals the meaning
 of that strife:

> "It was never
>  a mistake."

The Conflict-of-Law(s)
 was not error—
 it was the motion
 by which Reason
 revealed its structure.

Every contradiction
 marked a boundary.
 Every paradox
 showed where grasp must stop.

And the Ideas—
 Soul, World, God—
 though never Offered,
 kept the structure
 from splintering.

Their task
 was not to be found.
 But to hold
 what was being searched for.

Toil-Of now sees:

>   "The Whole
>    is not something
>    I can build.
>    But I must act
>    as if it must be built."

Reason's strife
 was the form
 of its own unity.

The Skill-Of-Judging-Lawfully
does not silence the Compass.
It does not dissolve
the tension.

It affirms it.

"You must seek
the Absolute—
not to possess it,
but so that
everything beneath it
does not collapse."

"The Unconditioned
was never Offered.
But it Must-Be-Imagined—
so that all which is Offered
may align."

Thus ends the conflict—
not by peace,
but by structure.

The Discipline of Pure Reason

Toil-Of
has strained, reached, collapsed—
and learned.

Now it must learn
to **hold**.

What once drove Reason
into illusion
must now be bound
by Rule.

For not all judgment
that follows form
is lawful.

Some are only shadows—
imitations of structure.

This is the danger:

**Pseudo-Skilled-Lawful-Judging**
speaks as if
it were Critique.
But it judges
without Offering.

It confuses speech
 with ground.
 It takes Form
 for Foundation.

It borrows
 the cadence of Reason,
 but not its constraints.

It speaks in syllogisms,
 but never asks:

> "Was anything
> truly given?"

The Skill-Of-Judging-Lawfully
 now draws the line:

> "To Judge
> is not merely
> to conclude."

> "It is to work
> within the Frame."

> "You may not build
> from inference
> alone."

Toil-Of
must now be trained—
not to silence Reason,
but to hold it
within the **form of law**.

For if Reason
continues without this discipline,
it becomes nothing
but motion:

>  convincing,
>    continuous,
>   and false.

True discipline
is not suppression.
It is structure.

And the structure
Must-Hold
for all lawful building
to proceed.

*Where Judgment Is Trained to Obey What It Cannot Grasp*

Toil-Of
  has learned
  not to leap.

But now it must learn
  not to *speak*
  beyond the Frame.

For Reason is tempted—
  always—
  to mimic the form
  of law.

It says:

>  "If it follows,
>    it must be true."

It arranges words
  into form,
  then calls the form
  a thing.

But The Skill-Of-Judging-Lawfully
  intervenes:

"Structure
is not substance."
"You cannot reason
your way
into Offering."

For true law
does not emerge
from persuasion.

It emerges
from obedience
to **That-Which-Is-Highest**.

And That-Which-Is-Highest
cannot be named,
only presupposed.

It does not give conclusions.
It gives **the condition**
under which conclusions
may lawfully appear.

Thus Reason must be trained
not to build
beyond the Gate—
but to speak
only in ways

aligned with
That-Which-Is-Highest.

Toil-Of
must now hold
every sentence
up to Judgment:

> "Is this Form
> grounded in what was Offered?"
> "Or is it only the appearance
> of lawfulness?"

Pseudo-Skilled-Lawful-Judging
always begins
in confidence.

True lawfulness
begins
in restraint.

---

## 🎭 *Where Toil-Of Must Not Confuse Motion with Ground*

Toil-Of
once believed
that to move was to know.

That if a concept could be traced
 from premise to conclusion,
 then something real
 had been found.

This is dogmatism:

> Reason, mistaking its **own law**
>  for **law itself.**

It builds castles
 from structure—
 then kneels before them.

But The Skill-Of-Judging-Lawfully
 draws the boundary:

> "To judge
>  is not to rule."
> "It is to obey
>  That-Which-Is-Highest."

For Offering
 does not emerge
 from deduction.
 And certainty
 does not follow
 from structure alone.

Dogmatism
  forgets the condition:

    That no Form
      may become Law
      unless it arises
      from the Offered.

And the Offered
  may only appear
  if the Frame
  has already been shaped
  by That-Which-Is-Highest.

So Reason
  must not invent.
  It must not decree.

It must align.
  It must reflect.
  It must hold form
  to structure,
  and structure
  to offering.

Toil-Of
  must not break
  its own Compass—
  by pretending

it invented
the direction it follows.

---

🎭 *Where Toil-Of Learns to Build Only with Offered Stone*

Toil-Of
now faces its mirror:

**Mathematics**—
the lawful builder.
**Metaphysics**—
the shadow that mimics building.

Mathematics does not overreach.
It stays within
what can be drawn
inside the Frame.

Every figure
must be constructed.
Every proof
must be plucked
from space,
from form,
from sequence.

Its truths arise
 not from assertion—
 but from **Offering**.

Metaphysics,
 when left undisciplined,
 speaks like mathematics—
 but draws
 from nothing.

It shapes
 without ground.
 It concludes
 without appearance.
 It constructs
 what was never Offered.

This is where
 Pseudo-Skilled-Lawful-Judging
 takes root—
 where language
 replaces law.

But The Skill-Of-Judging-Lawfully
 sets the line:

   "You may not build
    from concept alone."

"No Idea
may count as lawful
unless it appears
in accordance with
That-Which-Is-Highest."

Toil-Of
must learn to work
as mathematics does:

Slowly,
within the Form.
Never beyond the Gate.
Always within the Offering.

Metaphysics is not banished.
But it is bound—
not by silence,
but by **structure**.

And where it obeys
the compass of law
rather than the seduction of form—
it becomes
possible once again.

---

📖 Canon of Pure Reason

Toil-Of
can no longer grasp.
It can only stand.

And it asks—
not what exists,
but what **must-be-held**
for **acting** to be lawful.

The Skill-Of-Judging-Lawfully responds:

"You ask no longer
for Offering.
You ask what must
**already structure your Offering**
if you are to obey That-Which-Is-
Highest."

First appears:
**One's-Own-Law.**

Not a Negative-Freedom from—
but Positive-Freedom **within**:
the self as lawgiver
to itself.

No command from without.
No desire from below.
Only the **must-be-done**

that arises
because the Will
still longs
for structure.

The Compass still turns.
But now it draws
an inward arc.

Second appears:
**God**—
not as being,
but as **necessary projection**
of lawful completeness.

The frame of morality
demands a **summit**—
a place where Will and Law
are One.

We do not know God.
But if we obey Duty,
we must act
**as if God Must-Be**.

Third appears:
**Immortality**—
not as time eternal,

but as the **unending striving**
to become aligned.

For Duty demands
infinite motion.
And so the Toil
cannot rest
until the Self
becomes its Law.

These are not conclusions.
They are **presuppositions**—
projections
of That-Which-Is-Highest
onto action.

And in this
begins **Autonomous-Freedom**:
not escape from law,
but the joy
of being able
to make oneself
**a law**.

---

🎭 *Reason Draws the Line Between Knowing and Acting*

Toil-Of
begs for certainty.

It longs to grasp
what guides it.

But The-Skill-Of-Judging-Lawfully
holds the Compass steady:

"That-Which-Is-Highest
does not appear."
"It must-be-presupposed."

And so Reason
learns not to build castles—
but to walk
under open sky.

It may not say
"God is."
It may only say:

"If I am to act lawfully,
God Must-Be-There."

It may not say
"The soul endures."
But only:

"If I am to strive
toward perfection,
I must continue
without end."

Knowledge is denied.
But Orientation is preserved.

> "Do not grasp,"
> says the Compass.
> "Align."

> "Do not prove,"
> says the Frame.
> "Presuppose."

And in this discipline
arises the Commander's-Freedom:

> Not to command,
> but to obey
> One's-Own-Law
> in full awareness
> of That-Which-Is-Highest.

Toil-Of cannot climb
to heaven.
But it may build
a life
that **deserves** it.

## ☻ *Reason Declares Its Lawful Silence—Yet Acts with Certainty*

It may not say:
"God is."
It may only say:

"If I am to act
with integrity—
God Must-Be."

It may not say:
"I am immortal."
But only:

"If the Law within me
is infinite in scope—
then my striving
Must-Continue-Beyond-Measure."

And so
The-Skill-Of-Judging-Lawfully
does not judge to possess—
but judges
**to orient.**

Not to say what is—
but to hold
what Must-Be-There

for One's-Own-Law
to appear.

In this way,
 Reason stops pretending
 to know the Whole—
 and begins
 to walk with it.

Commander's-Freedom
 is not a conclusion.
 It is the beginning
 of the moral path.

And Reason
 becomes worthy
 of its name—
 not when it grasps,
 but when it obeys
 the Law
 it must give
 to itself.

---

☐ Architectonic of Pure Reason

Reason lifts its Compass.
 Not to draw illusions—

but to construct
the lawful Whole.

Toil-Of watches
 as the Frame appears:

    Not a pile of thoughts—
    but a Structure
    where every Offering
    must hold its place.

This is the Architectonic:
Reason becomes Builder
of That-Which-Is-Highest—
not in content,
but in lawful Form.

Each domain of knowledge
 finds its chamber.
 Each path of inquiry
 must anchor
 in the Foundation.

No fragment is allowed
 to stand alone.
 Philosophy
 must be a City
 with inner Law.

Even moral striving—
even One's-Own-Law—
must hold its place
within the Frame.

And so the Compass
returns to its Center—
not to possess Truth,
but to **construct**
what can lawfully
be offered.

Here ends the illusion
of scattered wisdom.
Here begins
the lawful Unity
of That-Which-Is-Highest.

---

📓 *The History of Pure Reason*

Toil-Of
began with hunger.
It saw motion
and thought:
"This Must-Lead-To-The-Origin."

It climbed
  as far as it could—
  and the Summit vanished.

It reached
  for That-Which-Is-Highest—
  and found
  only shadows
  drawn by its own hand.

It questioned Being—
  but offered no frame.
  It asked for Soul—
  but demanded a Thing.
  It posited God—
  but as an extension
  of appearance.

And so Reason
  mistook the Compass
  for a hand to hold.

>     It called itself metaphysician—
>       but it built no lawful City.
>       It called its illusions "Systems"—
>       but never measured
>       whether they could hold.

Now it sees:
the collapse
was lawful.
The contradiction
was a Signal.

All false structures
broke
against the boundary
of What-Cannot-Be-Grasped.

This is the History
of Pure Reason:

a journey from grasping
to law,
from assertion
to Offering,
from blindness
to That-Which-Is-Highest—
not known,
but lawfully Presupposed.

And now
Reason rests—not in silence,
but in Orientation.

It does not command.
It does not possess.

But it builds a Frame
in which the Law
of One's-Own-Law
may appear.

www.ingramcontent.com/pod-product-compliance
Lightning Source LLC
Chambersburg PA
CBHW081646270326
41933CB00018B/3369